CUPCAKE heaven

Susannah Blake

photography by Martin Brigdale

CUPCAKE

heaven

RYLAND
PETERS
& SMALL

LONDON NEW YORK

introduction

Who knows why cupcakes are so irresistible? Is it their individual size? Is it their delightful frostings and decorations? Is it their pretty paper liners? Or is it just that they're so darn cute? A whole, wickedly indulgent cake in miniature—all to yourself! Whatever the answer, the truth is undeniable—no one is able to resist their oh-so-sweet charms!

Cupcake time

The fabulous thing about cupcakes is that they really do suit any occasion—whether it's a sugary treat with midmorning coffee, a little something after your lunchtime sandwich, an indulgence to go with a cup of afternoon tea, a post-dinner dessert, or a little midnight feast before bed. And whatever time you bring them out, you will always be greeted with smiles of pleasure. Everyone loves a cupcake—and every time of day seems to be a cupcake time of day.

Simple pleasures

Cupcakes are fun to bake because they're just so easy. They require basic ingredients and equipment, and they take very little time to bake. The only thing that might take a little time is the decoration and even that is up to you. Some of the sweetest, prettiest cupcakes are the simplest after all. A spoonful of white glacé icing and a single raspberry or glacé cherry can look stunning—and can take no time at all. And although a sophisticated cupcake piled with a more complex frosting, chocolate curls, and chopped nuts might take a little longer, the result is so spectacular that you'll never mind putting in the extra effort.

Fun for adults, fun for kids

It's not just adults who can enjoy making and eating cupcakes. Kids can have a great time with them too. For younger children, you might want to make the cupcakes and frostings, then let the kids run wild sticking on plenty of decorations. Meanwhile, for older children, making, baking, and decorating the cupcakes under supervision will be a rewarding challenge—and a great activity for a rainy afternoon. Weighing, measuring, timing, and basic kitchen safety are all great skills to learn. Cooking with your kids is also a great way to have proper family time and really bond with them. Start them off with simpler recipes such as Passion Fruit Butterfly Cakes (pages 40–41) and Creamy Coconut Cupcakes (pages 26–27), or recipes from the Kids' Cupcakes chapter (pages 128–155).

ingredients

Although there are many variations on the classic cupcake, most cupcake mixtures are based on four basic ingredients: butter, sugar, eggs, and flour. Other ingredients such as chocolate, nuts, dried fruit, and other flavorings such as vanilla and grated lemon peel may then be stirred through the mixture to add texture and flavor.

Butter

For the best results, it is usually best to use unsalted butter for cupcakes. For creamed mixtures, where the butter and sugar are beaten together, the butter should be left at room temperature until soft. For people with a dairy intolerance or allergy, they may prefer to use a nondairy margarine in place of butter.

Sugar

The most common sugar for making cupcakes is granulated sugar, but other sugars and sweeteners may also be used, all of which add their own unique taste and texture. Brown sugars, honey, and syrups such as pure maple syrup will all add a distinctive flavor as well as sweetness to cakes. They will also affect the texture of the cakes. Honey and syrups are frequently heated before being used in cake mixtures such as the Gingerbread Cupcakes with Lemon Icing (pages 38–39).

Eggs

Used to enrich cakes, but also to bind the ingredients together, eggs are best used at room temperature. The eggs used in all the recipes in this book were medium.

Flour

Most cupcakes use self-rising flour or all-purpose flour with a little baking powder to help the cakes rise. However, other flours can also be used to make cupcakes—either on their own or combined with self-rising or all-purpose flour. Cornmeal, rice flour, and potato flour are all popular. Ground almonds are also frequently used in place of flour in cupcakes.

Additional ingredients

There are countless additional ingredients that you can fold into a basic cupcake mixture.

Fruit is always popular—whether dried or fresh. Small dried fruits such as golden raisins can be folded straight into the mixture, while larger fruits such as apricots will need to be chopped first. The same is true of fresh fruits. Blueberries and red currants can be folded in whole, while apples and pears should be peeled and chopped, and bananas might be mashed.

Nuts and seeds are other popular ingredients and may be added whole or chopped, depending on size. They add both flavor and texture.

You will also frequently use melted chocolate, marshmallows, coconut (dried, flaked, and creamed), stem ginger, and grated carrots.

Flavorings

There are many, many flavorings that may be added to cupcakes—and come in several forms including extracts, ground spices, citrus peels, and flavored sugars. Particularly popular flavorings include vanilla, coffee, chocolate, spices such as cinnamon and ginger, lemon peel, rosewater, and liqueurs and spirits.

The way you choose to top your cupcakes really is where the fun begins—apart from eating them of course! And the decorations are so many and varied as to cause endless delight. Simple or sophisticated, plain or indulgent, there really is a choice to suit every taste. From the simplest dusting of confectioners' sugar or drizzle of glacé icing, to swirls of rich buttercream, indulgent chocolate ganache, cool cream cheese frosting, and all manner of goodies to sprinkle and scatter on top. The choices really are endless.

Keeping it simple

The simplest of all decorations is a light dusting of either confectioners' sugar or cocoa powder. Cupcakes can also be decorated before baking with a sprinkling of slivered or chopped nuts, a little coarse sugar, or perhaps a slice or two of fresh apple or a piece of dried fruit. Plain, undecorated cupcakes keep for 2–3 days in an airtight container, but cupcakes with icings, frostings, or other embellishments should be eaten on the day.

Icings and frostings

Prettily colored, sugary sweet icings and frostings that you can drizzle, spoon, swirl, or pipe on top of cupcakes add a whole new dimension. Melted white or bittersweet chocolate, or a glacé icing made from confectioners' sugar and lemon juice are probably the simplest and are perfect for spooning or drizzling. Buttercreams, cream cheese frostings, chocolate ganaches, whipped cream, and creamy custards are more indulgent and excellent for swirling and piping.

decorating and embellishments

Sprinkles, candies, and other decorations

Once you've frosted your cupcake, you can leave it plain, but it's even more fun to add decorations. For simply decorated cupcakes, a whole nut, a glacé cherry, or a brightly colored candy can look stunning stuck in the center, right on top of a domed cupcake. But there are delightful colored sugar sprinkles that you can scatter all over frosted cupcakes—from sprinkles to tiny sugar shapes such as hearts, stars, and flowers. Other decorations include sugar and rice paper flowers, gold and silver dragées, edible sparkles, firework sparklers that you can light at the table, party candles, cocktail decorations that are perfect for sticking into cupcakes, fresh berries, and sugared rose petals. But look around. Supermarkets and kitchen stores are full of fabulous decorations and brightly colored candies that are perfect for decorating cupcakes. Let your imagination run wild and don't be afraid to experiment with the food coloring when tinting your frosting.

Fondant fancies

Fondant icing, which can be bought ready-made and ready-to-roll from the supermarket, is perfect for making sophisticated, professional-looking cupcakes. The icing can be colored with food coloring, then kneaded to incorporate the color, rolled out, cut into rounds, and draped over cupcakes to give a silky smooth finish. Decorations can then be added—or more icing can be molded into shapes to make funny faces such as the Pink Piggy Cupcakes (pages 130–131).

SIMPLE CUPCAKES

Blackberry, apple, and cinnamon are a sublime combination in these pretty little cupcakes. Studded with chunks of tender apple and warmly spiced with cinnamon, their moist, crumbly, melt-in-the-mouth taste and texture are offset perfectly by the sweet, sticky soured cream frosting.

APPLE AND CINNAMON CUPCAKES

6 tablespoons unsalted butter, at room temperature

½ cup granulated sugar

1 egg, beaten

½ cup sour cream

1¼ cups self-rising flour

¼ teaspoon baking soda

½ teaspoon ground cinnamon

1 eating apple, peeled, cored, and diced

to decorate

⅓ cup sour cream

about 1 cup confectioners' sugar, sifted

¼ teaspoon freshly squeezed lemon juice

about 36 blackberries

a 12-cup cupcake pan, lined with paper liners

makes 12

Preheat the oven to 350°F.

Beat the butter and sugar in a bowl until pale and creamy, then gradually beat in the egg. Stir in the sour cream. Combine the flour, baking soda, and cinnamon and sift into the mixture. Fold in, along with the apple.

Spoon the mixture into the paper liners and bake in the preheated oven for about 20 minutes until risen and golden and a skewer inserted in the center comes out clean. Transfer to a wire rack to cool.

To decorate, put the sour cream and sugar in a bowl and beat together for about 1 minute until smooth and creamy. Add a little more sugar if the frosting is not thick enough. Stir in the lemon juice. Spoon the frosting on top of the cupcakes and top each one with two or three blackberries.

Lightly spiced and topped with a creamy citrus mascarpone frosting, these delightful cupcakes are just the thing when you need a treat. They're not too sweet, but offer just the right combination of crunch, crumble, spice, sweetness, and creaminess—plus that little hint of naughtiness that a cupcake should always have.

CARROT AND CARDAMOM CUPCAKES

½ cup packed brown sugar

⅔ cup sunflower oil

2 eggs

grated peel of 1 unwaxed orange

seeds from 5 cardamom pods, crushed

½ teaspoon ground ginger

1½ cups self-rising flour

2 carrots, grated

½ cup shelled walnuts or pecans, roughly chopped

to decorate

⅔ cup mascarpone

finely grated peel of 1 unwaxed orange

1½ teaspoons freshly squeezed lemon juice

⅓ cup confectioners' sugar, sifted

a 12-cup cupcake pan, lined with paper liners

makes 12

Preheat the oven to 350°F.

Put the sugar in a bowl and break up using the back of a fork, then beat in the oil and eggs. Stir in the orange peel, crushed cardamom seeds, and ginger, then sift the flour into the mixture and fold in, followed by the carrot and nuts.

Spoon the mixture into the paper liners and bake in the preheated oven for about 20 minutes until risen and a skewer inserted in the center comes out clean. Transfer to a wire rack to cool.

To decorate, beat the mascarpone, orange peel, lemon juice, and sugar together in a bowl and spread over the cupcakes.

Dense and almondy with a sticky, chewy marzipan center, these sweet little cupcakes are the ideal choice for anyone with a sweet tooth who also likes the strong flavor of almonds. Pack a few in a pretty box as a gift for a sweet-toothed friend and watch them disappear in no time.

CHERRY AND MARZIPAN CUPCAKES

1 stick unsalted butter, at room temperature

½ cup granulated sugar

2 eggs

scant ¾ cup self-rising flour

⅓ cup ground almonds

½ cup glacé cherries, quartered

1 oz. marzipan, finely grated

to decorate

2 tablespoons freshly squeezed lemon juice

1⅔ cups confectioners' sugar, sifted

12 glacé cherries

a 12-cup cupcake pan, lined with paper liners

makes 12

Preheat the oven to 350°F.

Beat the butter and sugar together in a bowl until pale and fluffy, then beat in the eggs, one at a time. Sift the flour into the mixture and fold in, along with the ground almonds and glacé cherries.

Spoon small dollops of the mixture into the paper liners, sprinkle over some marzipan, and top with the remaining mixture. Bake in the preheated oven for about 18 minutes until risen and golden and a skewer inserted in the center comes out clean. Transfer to a wire rack to cool.

To decorate, put the lemon juice and sugar in a bowl and stir until smooth and creamy. Spoon on top of the cupcakes and top each one with a glacé cherry.

Subtly scented with lavender, these golden, buttery cupcakes are deliciously simple with an understated elegance, so they're perfect for serving midafternoon with a cup of tea. The fragrant taste of the lavender flowers gives the cupcakes an elusive hint that you can't quite put your finger on.

LAVENDER CUPCAKES

½ cup granulated sugar

¼ teaspoon dried lavender flowers

1 stick unsalted butter, at room temperature

2 eggs

1 cup self-rising flour

2 tablespoons milk

to decorate

1½ cups confectioners' sugar, sifted

1 egg white

lilac food coloring

12 sprigs of fresh lavender

a 12-cup cupcake pan, lined with paper liners

makes 12

Preheat the oven to 350°F.

Put the sugar and lavender flowers in a food processor and process briefly to combine. Tip the lavender sugar into a bowl with the butter and beat together until pale and fluffy.

Beat the eggs into the butter mixture, one at a time, then sift in the flour and fold in. Stir in the milk.

Spoon the mixture into the paper liners. Bake in the preheated oven for about 18 minutes until risen and golden and a skewer inserted in the center comes out clean. Transfer to a wire rack to cool.

To decorate, gradually beat the sugar into the egg white in a bowl, then add a few drops of food coloring and stir to achieve a lavender-color frosting. Spoon the frosting over the cupcakes, then top each one with a sprig of fresh lavender. Let set before serving.

Sweet with coconut and tangy with lime, these golden cupcakes with their snowy-white, ruffled tops look stunning arranged on a colored plate. Serve them midmorning with coffee, midafternoon with tea, or after dinner as a dessert. They are very easy to make and yet look so delightful that everyone will want to tuck in.

CREAMY COCONUT CUPCAKES

6 tablespoons unsalted butter, at room temperature

2 tablespoons coconut cream

½ cup granulated sugar

2 eggs

¾ cup self-rising flour

1 teaspoon baking powder

3 tablespoons dried coconut

grated peel of 1 unwaxed lime

2 tablespoons milk

to decorate

5 oz. cream cheese

⅓ cup confectioners' sugar, sifted

2 teaspoons freshly squeezed lime juice

coconut shavings

a 12-cup cupcake pan, lined with paper liners

makes 12

Preheat the oven to 350°F.

Beat the butter, coconut cream, and sugar together in a bowl until pale and fluffy, then beat in the eggs, one at a time. Sift the flour and baking powder into the mixture and fold in, then stir in the dried coconut and lime peel, followed by the milk.

Spoon the mixture into the paper liners, then bake in the preheated oven for about 17 minutes until risen and golden and a skewer inserted in the center comes out clean. Transfer to a wire rack to cool.

To decorate, beat the cream cheese, sugar, and lime juice together in a bowl. Swirl the frosting on top of the cupcakes, then sprinkle over coconut shavings in a thick layer.

Orange and poppyseed are a classic combination in these lusciously simple, tangy cupcakes. The luxuriously creamy mascarpone topping adds just the right edge of indulgence to the delicate citrus sponge speckled with tiny black poppyseeds. You might even convince yourself that these were fruity enough to have for breakfast!

ORANGE AND POPPYSEED CUPCAKES

1 stick unsalted butter, at room temperature

½ cup granulated sugar

2 eggs

1 cup self-rising flour

finely grated peel of 1 unwaxed orange

1 tablespoon poppyseeds

to decorate

2 oranges

8 oz. mascarpone

½ cup confectioners' sugar, sifted

a 12-cup cupcake pan, lined with paper liners

makes 12

Preheat the oven to 350°F.

Beat the butter and sugar together in a bowl until pale and fluffy, then beat in the eggs one at a time. Sift the flour into the mixture and fold in, then stir in the orange peel and poppyseeds.

Spoon the mixture into the paper liners and bake in the preheated oven for about 18 minutes until risen and golden and a skewer inserted into the center comes out clean. Transfer to a wire rack to cool.

To decorate, finely grate the peel from one of the oranges and set the peel aside. Put both the oranges on a cutting board and slice off the peel from the second orange and the white pith from both oranges. Cut between the membranes to remove the orange segments, then set aside.

Put the mascarpone, sugar, and reserved orange peel in a bowl and beat together until smooth and creamy. Swirl the frosting on top of the cupcakes, then decorate with orange segments.

Using yellow cornmeal gives these cupcakes a distinctive texture with an almost crispy bite and a gloriously rich color. Studded with juicy blueberries and topped with a rich, zesty cream cheese frosting, they offer the perfect pairing of light, fresh fruit and rich, creamy indulgence. Mouthwatering!

BLUEBERRY AND LEMON CUPCAKES

⅓ cup fine-ground yellow cornmeal

⅓ cup all-purpose flour

1 teaspoon baking powder

1 tablespoon crème fraîche or sour cream

1½ tablespoons sunflower oil

grated peel of 1 unwaxed lemon

1 tablespoon freshly squeezed lemon juice

1 egg

¼ cup granulated sugar

½ cup blueberries

to decorate

15 oz. cream cheese

⅔ cup confectioners' sugar, sifted

½ teaspoon grated unwaxed lemon peel

1 tablespoon freshly squeezed lemon juice

about ½ cup blueberries

strips of unwaxed lemon peel

a 12-cup cupcake pan, lined with just 10 paper liners

makes 10

Preheat the oven to 350°F.

Combine the cornmeal, flour, and baking powder in a bowl, then set aside. Beat the crème fraîche or sour cream, oil, lemon peel, and juice together in a small pitcher, then set aside.

In a separate bowl, beat the egg and sugar together for about 4 minutes until thick and pale, then add the lemon mixture and fold in. Sift the cornmeal mixture over the top and fold in to combine.

Spoon the mixture into the paper liners, then drop about 4 blueberries on top of each one, gently pressing them into the mixture. Bake in the preheated oven for 15–16 minutes until risen and golden and a skewer inserted in the center comes out clean. Transfer to a wire rack to cool.

To decorate, beat the cream cheese in a bowl until creamy, then beat in the sugar, lemon peel, and juice. Swirl big dollops of frosting on top of the cupcakes and decorate with fresh blueberries and strips of lemon peel.

Maple syrup and pecans are a classic combination, and no better anywhere than in these light, sticky cupcakes topped with creamy, buttery frosting and caramelized pecans. Look out for the dark amber maple syrup as it has a more intense flavor that really shines through in the fluffy, buttery cake.

MAPLE AND PECAN CUPCAKES

1 stick unsalted butter, at room temperature

¼ cup packed brown sugar

⅔ cup pure maple syrup

2 eggs

1 cup self-rising flour

½ cup shelled pecans, roughly chopped

to decorate

½ cup granulated sugar

12 pecan halves

3 tablespoons unsalted butter, at room temperature

3 tablespoons pure maple syrup

1¼ cups confectioners' sugar, sifted

a 12-cup cupcake pan, lined with paper liners

makes 12

Preheat the oven to 350°F.

Beat the butter and sugar together in a bowl until creamy, then beat in the maple syrup. Beat in the eggs, one at a time, then sift the flour into the mixture and fold in, along with the nuts.

Spoon the mixture into the paper liners and bake in the preheated oven for about 17 minutes until risen and golden and a skewer inserted in the center comes out clean. Transfer to a wire rack to cool.

To make the caramelized pecans, put the granulated sugar in a saucepan and add 2 tablespoons water. Heat gently, stirring, until the sugar melts and dissolves. Increase the heat and boil for about 6 minutes until it turns a pale gold color. Spread the nuts out on a sheet of parchment paper and spoon over a little of the caramel to cover each nut individually. Let cool.

Beat the butter, maple syrup, and confectioners' sugar together in a bowl until pale and fluffy. Spread the mixture over the cupcakes and top each one with a caramelized pecan.

Delicately scented with rosewater, these gorgeous pink cupcakes are perfect for girls who like things extra-pretty. I like pale pink sugared rose petals on mine, but darker pink or white will look just as lovely. For an extra indulgence, try stirring 2 oz. chopped Turkish delight into the cake mixture before spooning it into the paper liners.

ROSEWATER CUPCAKES

1 stick unsalted butter, at room temperature

½ cup granulated sugar

2 eggs

1 cup self-rising flour

1 tablespoon rosewater

to decorate

12 pink rose petals

1 egg white, beaten

1 tablespoon superfine sugar

1½–2 tablespoons freshly squeezed lemon juice

1¼ cups confectioners' sugar, sifted

red food coloring

a 12-cup cupcake pan, lined with paper liners

makes 12

Preheat the oven to 350°F.

Beat the butter and sugar together in a bowl until pale and fluffy, then beat in the eggs, one at a time. Sift the flour into the mixture and fold in, then stir in the rosewater.

Spoon the mixture into the paper liners and bake in the preheated oven for about 17 minutes until risen and golden and a skewer inserted in the center comes out clean. Transfer to a wire rack to cool.

To decorate, brush each rose petal with egg white, then sprinkle with the superfine sugar and let dry for about 1 hour.

Put 1½ tablespoons lemon juice in a bowl, then sift the confectioners' sugar into the bowl and stir until smooth. Add a little more lemon juice as required to make a smooth, spoonable frosting. Add one or two drops of food coloring to achieve a pale pink frosting, then drizzle over the cupcakes. Top each one with a sugared rose petal. Let set before serving.

These soft, sticky, dark brown cupcakes are dense and gingery, and delicious drizzled with a simple lemon icing. If you want elegant flat-topped cakes, make them in large liners, but if you prefer slightly domed cakes with icing drizzling down the sides, make them in regular-size liners.

GINGERBREAD CUPCAKES WITH LEMON ICING

4 tablespoons unsalted butter

¼ cup packed brown sugar

2 tablespoons light corn syrup

2 tablespoons dark molasses

1 teaspoon ground ginger

⅓ cup milk

1 egg, beaten

2 pieces of stem ginger in syrup, drained and chopped

1 cup self-rising flour

to decorate

2 tablespoons freshly squeezed lemon juice

1⅔ cup confectioners' sugar, sifted

2–3 pieces of stem ginger in syrup, drained and chopped

a 12-cup cupcake pan, lined with paper liners

makes 12

Preheat the oven to 325°F.

Put the butter, sugar, corn syrup, molasses, and ground ginger in a saucepan and heat gently until melted. Remove the pan from the heat and stir in the milk, then beat in the egg and stem ginger. Sift the flour into the mixture and fold in.

Spoon the mixture into the paper liners and bake in the preheated oven for about 20 minutes until risen and a skewer inserted in the center comes out clean. Transfer to a wire rack to cool.

To decorate, pour the lemon juice into a bowl. Gradually sift in the sugar, stirring as you go, until smooth, thick, and spoonable. Spoon the icing over the cupcakes and put a few pieces of stem ginger on each one. Let set before serving.

These sweet, sticky, crumbly cupcakes are divine and make a sophisticated alternative to the classic iced cupcake. They're particularly good served with a cup of fragrant tea such as jasmine, Earl Grey, or Lapsang Souchong. Make sure they are still warm when you serve them to enjoy them at their very best.

APRICOT, HONEY, AND PINE NUT CUPCAKES

5 tablespoons unsalted butter

3 tablespoons brown sugar

¼ cup honey

½ tablespoon milk

1 egg

¾ cup self-rising flour

1 oz. dried apricots, roughly chopped

2 tablespoons pine nuts

to decorate

4 tablespoons pine nuts, toasted

4 oz. dried apricots, roughly chopped

4 tablespoons honey

a 12-cup cupcake pan, lined with just 10 paper liners

makes 10

Preheat the oven to 350°F.

Put the butter, sugar, honey, and milk in a saucepan and warm over very gentle heat, stirring occasionally until melted. Remove from the heat and let cool for 5 minutes.

Beat the egg into the warm mixture, then stir in the flour. Fold in the apricots and pine nuts.

Spoon the mixture into the paper liners and bake in the preheated oven for 15 minutes until risen and golden and a skewer inserted in the center comes out clean. Transfer to a wire rack.

To decorate, put the pine nuts, apricots, and honey in a small saucepan and warm gently over low heat. Stir until the honey has melted and the apricots and pine nuts are well coated. Spoon the mixture over the cupcakes and serve warm.

A plateful of these pretty, passion fruit-scented cakes look like a swarm of fluttering butterflies. They remind me of the children's tea parties of my youth, where you were guaranteed to find a batch of butterfly cakes clustered on the tea table. So these are perfect for the child in us all!

PASSION FRUIT BUTTERFLY CAKES

3 passion fruit

1 stick unsalted butter, at room temperature

½ cup granulated sugar

2 eggs

1 cup self-rising flour

1 teaspoon baking powder

to decorate

6 passion fruit

⅔ cup mascarpone

4 tablespoons confectioners' sugar, sifted, plus extra to dust

a 12-cup cupcake pan, lined with paper liners

makes 12

Preheat the oven to 350°F.

Halve the passion fruit and scoop the flesh into a strainer set over a bowl. Press with the back of a teaspoon to extract the juice.

Beat the butter and sugar together in a bowl until pale and fluffy, then beat in the eggs, one at a time. Sift the flour and baking powder into the mixture and fold in. Stir in the passion fruit juice.

Spoon the mixture into the paper liners, then bake in the preheated oven for about 17 minutes until risen and golden and a skewer inserted in the center comes out clean. Transfer to a wire rack to cool.

To decorate, halve the passion fruit and scoop the flesh into a strainer set over a bowl. Press with the back of a teaspoon to extract the juice, then add the mascarpone and sugar to the bowl. Mix until smooth and creamy. Cover and refrigerate for about 30 minutes to thicken up.

Slice the top off each cupcake, then cut each top in half. Spoon a generous dollop of the mascarpone mixture onto each cupcake, then top with the two halves, setting them at an angle to resemble wings. Dust with confectioners' sugar and serve.

With a pale green crumb and a subtle taste of pistachio, these little cupcakes are utterly irresistible and unbelievably girly (which is just the way they should be)! To achieve a pale pistachio-color icing, use a light green food coloring if you can find one, adding a little at a time until you achieve just the right shade.

PISTACHIO CUPCAKES

⅓ cup shelled pistachio nuts

1 stick unsalted butter, at room temperature

½ cup granulated sugar

2 eggs

¾ cup self-rising flour

2 tablespoons milk

to decorate

1 egg white

1½ cups confectioners' sugar

¾ teaspoon freshly squeezed lemon juice

green food coloring

12 pink rice paper roses

a 12-cup cupcake pan, lined with paper liners

makes 12

Preheat the oven to 350°F.

Put the pistachio nuts in a food processor and process until finely ground. Set aside.

Beat the butter and sugar together in a bowl until pale and fluffy, then beat in the eggs, one at a time. Stir in the ground nuts, then sift the flour into the mixture and fold in. Stir in the milk.

Spoon the mixture into the paper liners. Bake in the preheated oven for about 18 minutes until risen and golden and a skewer inserted in the center comes out clean. Transfer to a wire rack to cool.

To decorate, put the egg white in a bowl and gradually sift over the sugar, beating in as you go until thick and glossy, then beat in the lemon juice. The icing should be thick but spoonable.

Add a few drops of food coloring to the icing and beat to make a pale pistachio-green icing. Spoon on top of the cupcakes and top each one with a pink rice paper rose. Let set before serving.

CELEBRATION
CUPCAKES

Who wants an old-fashioned tiered wedding cake when you could have a mountain of these pretty white wedding cupcakes instead? I like the white look when it comes to decorations, but you can add food coloring, flowers, or ribbon according to your color scheme. You can also use larger muffin pans to make a variety of sizes.

WEDDING CUPCAKES

1 stick unsalted butter, at room temperature

½ cup granulated sugar

2 eggs

1 cup self-rising flour

1 teaspoon pure vanilla extract or grated unwaxed lemon peel

2 tablespoons milk

to decorate

white lace or organza ribbon

1 egg white

1 cup confectioners' sugar, sifted

½ teaspoon freshly squeezed lemon juice

white edible flower decorations

a 12-cup cupcake pan, lined with paper liners

makes 12

Preheat the oven to 350°F.

Beat the butter and sugar together in a bowl until pale and fluffy, then beat in the eggs, one at a time. Sift the flour into the mixture and fold in. Stir in the vanilla extract or lemon peel and the milk.

Spoon the mixture into the paper liners and bake in the preheated oven for about 18 minutes until risen and golden and a skewer inserted in the center comes out clean. Transfer to a wire rack to cool.

To decorate, carefully tie a piece of ribbon around each cupcake. Put the egg white in a large bowl, then beat in the sugar until thick and creamy. Beat in the lemon juice to make a thick, spoonable frosting. (If necessary, add a drizzle more lemon juice or a little more sugar to get the right consistency.)

Spoon the frosting onto the cupcakes, then top each one with a flower. The frosting hardens quite fast, so work quickly as soon as you've made the frosting.

These sparkling cupcakes are perfect for an engagement party—or any celebration! Or for the true romantic, why not whip up a batch ready to propose with? Choose any shade of food coloring you like for the frosting and you can adapt these cupcakes to suit any number of glamorous occasions.

SPARKLING DIAMOND CUPCAKES

1 stick unsalted butter, at room temperature

½ cup granulated sugar

2 eggs

1 cup self-rising flour

3 pieces of stem ginger in syrup, drained and chopped

grated peel of 1 unwaxed lime

to decorate

about 6 clear mints

2½ tablespoons freshly squeezed lime juice

1⅓ cups confectioners' sugar, sifted

pale blue food coloring

edible clear sparkles

a 12-cup cupcake pan, lined with silver paper liners

makes 12

Preheat the oven to 350°F.

Beat the butter and sugar together in a bowl until pale and fluffy, then beat in the eggs, one at a time. Sift the flour into the mixture and fold in, then stir in the ginger and lime peel.

Spoon the mixture into the paper liners, then bake in the preheated oven for about 17 minutes until risen and golden and a skewer inserted in the center comes out clean. Transfer to a wire rack and let cool completely.

To decorate, leave the mints in their wrapper and tap with a rolling pin to break into pieces. Set aside.

Put the lime juice in a bowl, then sift the confectioners' sugar into the bowl and stir until smooth. Add a little more lime juice as required to make a smooth, spoonable frosting. Add a couple of drops of food coloring and stir in to achieve a pale blue color.

Spoon the frosting on top of the cupcakes. Pile a little heap of mint "diamonds" on each cupcake and sprinkle with edible sparkles.

Bake a batch of these delightfully flirtatious cupcakes filled with a zesty lemon cream and fresh raspberries for the one you love, and they'll never have eyes for anyone but you! For that extra-special touch, buy a cupcake pan with heart-shape cups and push your regular paper liners into the cups.

RASPBERRY LOVE-HEART CUPCAKES

1 stick unsalted butter, at room temperature

½ cup granulated sugar

2 eggs

1 cup self-rising flour

grated peel and freshly squeezed juice of ½ unwaxed lemon

to decorate

⅓ cup crème fraîche or sour cream

1 tablespoon jarred lemon curd

⅔ cup raspberries

confectioners' sugar, for dusting

a 12-cup cupcake pan (with heart-shape cups if you can find one), lined with paper liners

a mini heart-shape cookie cutter

makes 12

Preheat the oven to 350°F.

Beat the butter and sugar together in a bowl until pale and fluffy, then beat in the eggs, one at a time. Sift the flour into the mixture and fold in, then stir in the lemon peel and juice.

Spoon the mixture into the paper liners and bake in the preheated oven for about 18 minutes until risen and golden and a skewer inserted in the center comes out clean. Transfer to a wire rack to cool.

To decorate, using a sharp, pointed knife, remove a deep round from the center of each cupcake, just over 1 inch in diameter. Slice the pointed bit off each piece of cored-out cupcake so that you are left with a disk. Using the mini heart-shape cookie cutter, cut the disks into hearts.

Combine the crème fraîche or sour cream and lemon curd in a bowl, then fold in the raspberries. Spoon the mixture into the hollowed-out cupcakes, then top with the hearts. Dust generously with confectioners' sugar.

Pears and cranberries are classic seasonal Christmas fruits and nowhere better than in these moist, lightly spiced cupcakes topped with a luscious brandy butter. If you're baking the cupcakes for people who don't like the taste of brandy, substitute milk for the brandy and add 1 teaspoon pure vanilla extract.

PEAR AND CRANBERRY CHRISTMAS CUPCAKES

4 tablespoons unsalted butter, at room temperature

½ cup granulated sugar

2 eggs

1 cup self-rising flour

½ teaspoon apple pie spice

1 pear, peeled, cored, and diced

¼ cup dried cranberries

to decorate

6½ tablespoons unsalted butter, at room temperature

1 cup confectioners' sugar, sifted

4 teaspoons brandy

about 36 fresh cranberries

12 small holly leaves (optional)

edible gold balls (dragées)

a 12-cup cupcake pan, lined with paper liners

makes 12

Preheat the oven to 350°F.

Beat the butter and sugar together in a bowl until pale and fluffy, then beat in the eggs, one at a time. Sift the flour and apple pie spice into the mixture and fold in, then stir in the diced pear and dried cranberries.

Spoon the mixture into the paper liners and bake in the preheated oven for about 18 minutes until risen and golden and a skewer inserted in the center comes out clean. Transfer to a wire rack to cool.

To decorate, put the butter, sugar, and brandy in a bowl and beat together until smooth and creamy. Swirl the frosting on top of the cupcakes, then decorate each one with two or three fresh cranberries, a holly leaf, if using, and sprinkle with gold balls.

Sweet, spicy pumpkin cupcakes topped with pretty white and bittersweet chocolate cobwebs are definitely a treat rather than a trick. You can let the topping set completely if you like, but they're so much better when it's still soft. Around October you should be able to find spooky paper liners in specialist kitchen shops.

HALLOWEEN CUPCAKES

½ cup packed brown sugar

½ cup sunflower oil

2 eggs

1 cup grated pumpkin or butternut squash

grated peel of 1 unwaxed lemon

1 cup self-rising flour

1 teaspoon baking powder

1 teaspoon ground cinnamon

to decorate

5 oz. white chocolate, chopped

1 oz. bittersweet chocolate

a 12-cup cupcake pan, lined with paper liners

makes 12

Preheat the oven to 350°F.

Put the sugar in a bowl and break up with the back of a fork, then beat in the oil and eggs. Fold in the grated pumpkin and lemon peel. Combine the flour, baking powder, and cinnamon in a bowl, then sift into the mixture and fold in.

Spoon the mixture into the paper liners and bake in the preheated oven for about 18 minutes until risen and a skewer inserted in the center comes out clean. Transfer to a wire rack to cool.

To decorate, put the white and bittersweet chocolates in separate heatproof bowls set over pans of gently simmering water. Do not let the bowls touch the water. Leave until almost melted. Remove from the heat and let cool for about 5 minutes, then spoon the white chocolate over the cupcakes.

Cut a large square of parchment paper and fold into eighths to make a cone and tape together. Spoon the dark chocolate into the cone and snip the tip off so that you can pipe a thin line of chocolate. Put a dot of chocolate in the center of each cupcake, then pipe three concentric circles around the dot.

Using a skewer, draw a line from the central dot to the outside edge of the cupcake and repeat about eight times all the way round to create a spider's web pattern. Serve while the chocolate is still slightly soft and gooey.

For anyone who loves chewy, fruit-rich florentine cookies, these cupcakes offer the perfect combination, but in a cuter, more colorful package. A rich, white chocolate crumb is finished with glacé fruits, nuts, and a sticky white chocolate topping. Offer them to a friend who needs cheering up and watch their face light up!

FLORENTINE CUPCAKES

2 oz. white chocolate, chopped

1 stick unsalted butter, at room temperature

½ cup granulated sugar

2 eggs

1 cup self-rising flour

½ teaspoon pure vanilla extract

to decorate

3 oz. white chocolate, chopped

4 tablespoons heavy cream

1¾ oz. glacé fruits, such as citrus peel, apricots, pineapple, and angelica, chopped

6 glacé cherries, chopped

1¾ oz. shelled nuts, such as walnuts, pistachios, and hazelnuts, chopped

1 oz. slivered almonds (optional)

two 12-cup mini-cupcake pans or a baking sheet, plus 24 petits fours liners

makes 24

Preheat the oven to 350°F, then line the mini-cupcake pan with petit fours liners. (If you don't have a mini-cupcake pan, arrange the cases on a baking sheet; the cases should be able to cope with such a small amount of mixture.)

Put the chocolate in a heatproof bowl set over a pan of gently simmering water. Do not let the bowl touch the water. Leave until almost melted, then set aside to cool slightly.

Beat together the butter and sugar in a bowl until pale and fluffy, then beat in the eggs, one at a time. Sift the flour into the mixture and fold in, then stir in the vanilla extract and melted chocolate.

Spoon the mixture into the petits fours liners and bake in the preheated oven for about 18 minutes until golden and a skewer inserted in the center comes out clean. Transfer to a wire rack to cool.

To decorate, put the chocolate and cream in a heatproof bowl set over a pan of gently simmering water. Do not let the bowl touch the water. Leave until the chocolate is just starting to melt, then remove from the heat and stir until smooth. Stir in the glacé fruits and the nuts, then refrigerate for 20 minutes before spooning on top of the cupcakes. Decorate with slivered almonds, if using.

When you're desperate for a week on a desert island but haven't got the time or money, try one of these cupcakes instead. They may not be quite the same as a tropical holiday, but the dense little pineapple cakes smothered in rich, creamy coconut frosting and topped with sweet, juicy wedges of mango come in a fabulous second best!

TROPICAL CUPCAKES

6 tablespoons unsalted butter, at room temperature

½ cup packed brown sugar

2 eggs

4 tablespoons crème fraîche or sour cream

1 cup self-rising flour

¼ teaspoon apple pie spice

5 oz. canned pineapple, diced

to decorate

⅔ cup mascarpone

2 tablespoons coconut cream

⅓ cup confectioners' sugar, sifted

1 mango, pitted, peeled, and cut into wedges

a 12-cup cupcake pan, lined with paper liners

makes 12

Preheat the oven to 350°F.

Beat the butter and sugar together in a bowl until pale and fluffy, then beat in the eggs, one at a time. Stir in the crème fraîche or sour cream, then sift the flour and apple pie spice over the top and fold in. Add the pineapple and fold in.

Spoon the mixture into the paper liners and bake in the preheated oven for about 20 minutes until risen and golden and a skewer inserted in the center comes out clean. Transfer to a wire rack to cool.

To decorate, put the mascarpone, coconut cream, and sugar in a bowl and beat together until smooth and creamy. Swirl the frosting on top of the cupcakes and decorate with wedges of mango.

Topped with a cool, creamy mascarpone topping and golden shards of praline, these cupcakes offer a pure taste of heaven. A hint of bitter coffee brings out and enhances the flavor of the nutty praline. If you're a real coffee fiend, try one of these cupcakes with a cup of strong, black coffee.

COFFEE AND PRALINE CUPCAKES

½ cup granulated sugar

scant ½ cup blanched hazelnuts

1 stick unsalted butter, at room temperature

2 eggs

⅔ cup self-rising flour

1 teaspoon baking powder

2 teaspoons instant coffee, dissolved in 1 tablespoon boiling water

to decorate

2 tablespoons granulated sugar

¼ cup blanched hazelnuts, roughly chopped

scant ½ cup mascarpone

1 scant cup confectioners' sugar, sifted

1 teaspoon instant coffee, dissolved in ½ tablespoon boiling water

a 12-cup cupcake pan, lined with paper liners

makes 12

Preheat the oven to 350°F. Line a baking sheet with parchment paper.

Put half the sugar in a saucepan and heat gently, stirring, for about 5 minutes until melted and pale gold. Add the hazelnuts and cook, stirring, for about 1 minute, then pour onto the lined baking sheet and let harden for at least 20 minutes.

Break the hardened praline into pieces and place in a food processor, then process until finely ground. Set aside.

Beat the butter and the remaining sugar together in a bowl until pale and fluffy, then beat in the ground praline. Beat in the eggs, one at a time, then sift the flour and baking powder into the mixture and fold in. Stir in the coffee.

Spoon the mixture into the paper liners and bake in the preheated oven for about 16 minutes until risen and golden and a skewer inserted in the center comes out clean. Transfer to a wire rack to cool.

To decorate, put the granulated sugar in a saucepan and heat gently, stirring, for about 5 minutes until melted and pale gold. Add the hazelnuts and cook, stirring, for about 30 seconds, then pour onto the lined baking sheet. Let harden for about 20 minutes, then break into small shards.

Beat the mascarpone and confectioners' sugar together in a bowl until smooth and creamy, then stir in the coffee. Swirl the mixture onto the cupcakes and decorate with shards of praline.

These cupcakes, made using a classic génoise sponge mixture, are light and creamy and perfect for serving in summer when fresh soft berries are sweet and juicy. Experiment with any ripe berries you can find. Because the batter contains no fat, the cupcakes don't keep well, so they are best eaten on the day they're made.

FRESH FRUIT CUPCAKES

2 eggs

5 tablespoons granulated sugar

1 teaspoon pure vanilla extract

¾ cup all-purpose flour

to decorate

⅔ cup heavy cream

1 pint fresh summer berries, such as strawberries, blueberries, raspberries, and red currants

confectioners' sugar, for dusting

a 12-cup cupcake pan, lined with paper liners

makes 12

Preheat the oven to 350°F.

Put the eggs and sugar in a large bowl and beat for about 10 minutes until thick and pale. Add the vanilla extract. Sift the flour into a separate bowl twice, then sift into the egg mixture and fold in.

Spoon the mixture into the paper liners and bake in the preheated oven for about 12 minutes until risen and golden and a skewer inserted in the center comes out clean. Transfer to a wire rack to cool.

To decorate, whip the cream in a bowl until it stands in peaks, then swirl over the cupcakes. Top with fresh berries, dust with confectioners' sugar, and serve immediately.

These rich, dark, chocolatey cupcakes studded with chocolate-covered coffee beans and topped with a creamy coffee-butter frosting are simply divine. Dusted with grated chocolate, they look like a plateful of mini-cappuccinos—but don't eat too many or they might keep you awake all night!

CHOCA-MOCHA CUPCAKES

3 oz. bittersweet chocolate, chopped

10 tablespoons unsalted butter, at room temperature

¾ cup granulated sugar

2 eggs

2 tablespoons unsweetened cocoa powder

¾ cup self-rising flour

2 teaspoons instant coffee, dissolved in 1 tablespoon boiling water

¼ cup chocolate-covered coffee beans

to decorate

7 tablespoons unsalted butter, at room temperature

1⅔ cups confectioners' sugar, sifted

2 teaspoons instant coffee, dissolved in 1 tablespoon boiling water

bittersweet chocolate, grated

a 12-cup cupcake pan, lined with paper liners

makes 12

Preheat the oven to 350°F.

Put the chocolate in a heatproof bowl set over a pan of gently simmering water. Do not let the bowl touch the water. Leave until almost melted, then set aside to cool slightly.

Beat the butter and sugar together in a bowl until pale and fluffy, then beat in the eggs, one at a time. Stir in the melted chocolate and cocoa powder. Sift the flour into the mixture and stir in, then stir in the coffee, followed by the coffee beans.

Spoon the mixture into the paper liners and bake in the preheated oven for about 20 minutes until risen and a skewer inserted in the center comes out clean. Transfer to a wire rack to cool.

To decorate, beat the butter, sugar, and coffee together in a bowl until pale and fluffy. Spread the mixture smoothly over the cupcakes and sprinkle with grated chocolate.

Inspired by the classic Black Forest cake, these dinky, crumbly chocolate cupcakes are studded with sweet, sticky cherries and spiked with kirsch. If you really want to go overboard on indulgence, serve them topped with a dollop of whipped cream as well, and shave over some bittersweet chocolate curls.

BLACK FOREST CUPCAKES

3 oz. bittersweet chocolate, chopped

1 stick unsalted butter, at room temperature

½ cup granulated sugar

2 eggs

2 tablespoons ground almonds

1¼ cups self-rising flour

1 tablespoon unsweetened cocoa powder

2 tablespoons kirsch

½ cup glacé cherries, halved

to decorate

3½ oz. bittersweet chocolate, finely chopped, plus extra to decorate

½ cup heavy cream

1 tablespoon kirsch

12 glacé cherries

a 12-cup cupcake pan, lined with paper liners

makes 12

Preheat the oven to 350°F.

Put the chocolate in a heatproof bowl set over a pan of gently simmering water. Do not let the bowl touch the water. Leave until almost melted, then set aside to cool slightly.

Beat the butter and sugar together in a bowl until pale and fluffy, then beat in the eggs, one at a time. Beat in the melted chocolate, then stir in the almonds. Sift the flour and cocoa powder into the mixture and fold in, followed by the kirsch and the glacé cherries.

Spoon the mixture into the paper liners and bake in the preheated oven for about 20 minutes until a skewer inserted in the center comes out clean. Transfer to a wire rack to cool.

To decorate, put the chocolate in a heatproof bowl. Heat the cream in a saucepan until almost boiling, then pour over the chocolate and let melt for about 5 minutes. Stir until smooth and creamy, then stir in the kirsch and let cool for about 1 hour until thick and glossy. Spread the frosting over the cupcakes and top with a glacé cherry. Using a vegetable peeler, make some chocolate shavings with the extra bittersweet chocolate and pop them on top of the cupcakes.

Topped with a rich, gooey, sticky frosting, these wickedly dense, chocolatey cupcakes studded with chunks of sweet, peppery stem ginger are the only cupcake choice for ginger-loving chocaholics. Expecting friends round for tea? Surprise them by whipping up a batch of these irresistible little treats.

CHOCOLATE AND GINGER CUPCAKES

3 oz. bittersweet chocolate, chopped

6½ tablespoons unsalted butter, at room temperature

scant ½ cup granulated sugar

2 eggs

1 cup self-rising flour

2 tablespoons unsweetened cocoa powder

3 balls of stem ginger in syrup, drained and chopped

to decorate

3½ oz. bittersweet chocolate, finely chopped

1¾ oz. white marshmallows, snipped into pieces

½ cup heavy cream

a 12-cup cupcake pan, lined with paper liners

makes 12

Preheat the oven to 350°F.

Put the chocolate in a heatproof bowl set over a pan of gently simmering water. Do not let the bowl touch the water. Leave until almost melted, then set aside to cool for about 5 minutes.

Beat the butter and sugar together until pale and fluffy, then beat in the eggs, one at a time. Stir in the melted chocolate, then sift the flour and cocoa powder into the mixture and fold in. Add the ginger and stir in.

Spoon the mixture into the paper liners and bake in the preheated oven for about 18 minutes until a skewer inserted in the center comes out clean. Transfer to a wire rack to cool.

To decorate, put half the chocolate and the marshmallows in a heatproof bowl and set over a pan of barely simmering water. Heat gently, stirring occasionally, until the chocolate and marshmallows are almost melted. Remove the bowl from the heat and continue stirring until the marshmallows are completely melted.

Add the remaining chocolate and stir until melted, then stir in the cream. Let cool for about 2 hours until thick, then swirl on top of the cupcakes.

Inspired by the English classic, banoffee pie, these creamy cupcakes are to die for. The tender, moist banana cakes are packed with nuggets of chewy caramel, then topped with whipped cream, sweet and sticky dulce de leche, and fresh banana. You can make your own dulce de leche by following the instructions below.

BANOFFEE CUPCAKES

4 tablespoons unsalted butter, at room temperature

⅓ cup packed brown sugar

1 egg, beaten

1 ripe banana, mashed

1 cup self-rising flour

4 chewy caramels, chopped

to decorate

⅔ cup heavy cream, whipped

3–4 tablespoons dulce de leche or caramel sauce

1 banana, sliced

a 12-cup cupcake pan, lined with just 10 paper liners

makes 10

Preheat the oven to 350°F.

Beat the butter and sugar together in a bowl until creamy, then beat in the egg, a little at a time. Fold in the mashed banana, then sift the flour into the mixture and fold in, followed by the caramels.

Spoon the mixture into the paper liners and bake in the preheated oven for about 16 minutes until risen and a skewer inserted in the center comes out clean. Transfer to a wire rack to cool.

To decorate, swirl the cream over each of the cupcakes, then drizzle with a spoonful of dulce de leche or caramel sauce and top with slices of banana.

Note: Dulce de leche is a sweet caramel sauce from Argentina and it is available from larger supermarkets. If you can't find it, you can make it yourself. Put a sealed can of condensed milk in a saucepan, pour over boiling water to cover, and boil for 3 hours, adding more water as necessary so that the can is always covered. Remove from the pan and let cool completely before opening using a can opener. Stir well to make a smooth sauce before spooning over the cakes.

CUPCAKES
FOR SPECIAL DIETS

Perfect for anyone on a dairy-free diet, these tender cupcakes are delicately scented with fragrant cardamom and pistachio and drenched in a tangy, intensely flavored sticky lime syrup. The zucchini may sound like an odd ingredient but it gives the cupcakes a wonderfully moist texture.

ZUCCHINI, PISTACHIO, AND LIME CUPCAKES

seeds from 3 cardamom pods, crushed

1 egg

½ cup sunflower oil

scant ½ cup granulated sugar

3½ oz. zucchini, grated

scant ½ cup shelled pistachio nuts, chopped

1 cup self-rising flour

½ teaspoon baking powder

to decorate

finely grated peel and freshly squeezed juice of 2 unwaxed limes

7 tablespoons granulated sugar

⅓ cup shelled pistachio nuts, chopped

a 12-cup cupcake pan, lined with paper liners

makes 12

Preheat the oven to 325°F.

Put the crushed cardamom seeds in a bowl with the egg, oil, and sugar, then beat until smooth and creamy. Add the zucchini and nuts and stir together until well mixed. Combine the flour and baking powder, then sift into the zucchini mixture and fold in.

Spoon the mixture into the paper liners and bake in the preheated oven for 18–20 minutes until risen and golden and a skewer inserted in the center comes out clean. Transfer to a wire rack to cool.

To decorate, put the lime peel and juice, and the sugar into a saucepan. Heat gently, stirring, until the sugar has dissolved, then bring to a boil. Boil for about 1 minute, then remove from the heat. Stir in the nuts and let cool slightly until the syrup starts to thicken, then spoon over the cupcakes.

Naturally gluten-free, these light chocolate cupcakes made with potato flour and spread with a rich chocolate cream cheese frosting are great for anyone following a gluten- or nut-free diet. Top them with grated chocolate for a sophisticated treat, or sprinkle with edible sparkles for something more playful.

CHOCOLATE CREAM CHEESE CUPCAKES

3 tablespoons unsalted butter, melted

1 tablespoon unsweetened cocoa powder

½ cup granulated sugar

1 oz. cream cheese

1 egg

½ teaspoon pure vanilla extract

generous ⅓ cup potato flour

½ teaspoon baking powder

¼ teaspoon baking soda

1 tablespoon milk

to decorate

1 oz. bittersweet chocolate, plus extra to decorate

5 oz. cream cheese

⅓ cup confectioners' sugar, sifted

¼ teaspoon pure vanilla extract

a 12-cup cupcake pan, lined with paper liners

makes 12

Preheat the oven to 350°C.

In a bowl, stir together the butter and cocoa powder, then stir in the sugar. Add the cream cheese and beat in. Beat in the egg, then stir in the vanilla extract. Add the flour, baking powder, and baking soda and stir together. Stir in the milk.

Spoon the mixture into the paper liners and bake in the preheated oven for about 16 minutes until risen and a skewer inserted in the center comes out clean. Transfer to a wire rack to cool.

To decorate, put the chocolate in a heatproof bowl set over a pan of gently simmering water. Do not let the bowl touch the water. Leave until almost melted. Remove from the heat and let cool for about 10 minutes.

Beat together the melted chocolate, cream cheese, sugar, and vanilla extract until creamy, then spread the frosting on top of the cupcakes. Using a vegetable peeler, make chocolate shavings and scatter on top of the cupcakes.

Almost like the Scottish mini-Dundee cakes, these rich cupcakes flavored with brandy are a great gluten-free choice when you need a midafternoon treat with a cup of tea. At Christmas-time, you could leave off the almonds and decorate with marzipan, royal icing, and a sprig of holly or a festive snowman if you like.

RICH FRUIT CUPCAKES

4 tablespoons unsalted butter, at room temperature

3 tablespoons light brown sugar

1 egg, beaten

½ cup rice flour

1 teaspoon baking powder

2 tablespoons ground almonds

1 tablespoon brandy

¾ cup luxury mixed dried fruit

¼ cup blanched almonds

a 12-cup cupcake pan, lined with paper liners

makes 12

Preheat the oven to 325°F.

Beat together the butter and sugar in a bowl until smooth and creamy, then gradually beat in the egg. Combine the flour and baking powder, then sift into the mixture. Stir in, followed by the ground almonds, brandy, and dried fruit.

Spoon the mixture into the paper liners and top each cupcake with three or four blanched almonds. Bake in the preheated oven for 25 minutes until a skewer inserted in the center comes out clean. Transfer to a wire rack to cool.

Moist and chewy with a subtly spiced crumb and a simple orange icing, these cupcakes are best eaten on the day you make them. With their seasonal pumpkin filling and orange appearance, they would be perfect served at a Halloween party or as a healthier alternative to the usual "trick or treat" candies.

LOW-FAT PUMPKIN AND RICOTTA CUPCAKES

1 cup diced pumpkin or butternut squash

1 generous cup all-purpose flour

1½ teaspoons baking powder

½ cup granulated sugar

¼ teaspoon ground cinnamon

1 egg

2 tablespoons sunflower oil

½ cup low-fat milk

½ teaspoon pure vanilla extract

¼ cup part-skim ricotta

to decorate

2 tablespoons freshly squeezed orange juice

1⅔ cups confectioners' sugar, sifted

grated unwaxed orange peel

a 12-cup cupcake pan, lined with paper liners

makes 12

Preheat the oven to 400°C.

Put the pumpkin on a square of aluminum foil and fold up the edges to seal. Bake in the preheated oven for about 20 minutes until tender. Tip out into a bowl and mash roughly with a fork.

Reduce the oven temperature to 350°F.

Combine the flour, baking powder, sugar, and cinnamon and sift together into a bowl. In a separate bowl, combine the egg, oil, milk, vanilla extract, and ricotta and beat together until smooth. Stir in the mashed pumpkin. Pour into the dry ingredients and fold together until just combined.

Spoon the mixture into the paper liners and bake in the preheated oven for about 25 minutes until risen and a skewer inserted in the center comes out clean. Transfer to a wire rack and let cool.

To decorate, put the orange juice in a bowl, then sift the sugar into the bowl and stir until smooth. Spoon on top of the cupcakes and sprinkle with grated orange peel.

Bake up a batch of these cupcakes for vegan friends, or anyone following a nut-, egg- or dairy-free diet. The dark chocolate cupcakes with a hint of coffee are a delicious combination of soft crumb and sweet, fudgy frosting. They're so mouthwatering that everyone will love them, whatever their diet!

DARK CHOCOLATE CUPCAKES

1 cup all-purpose flour

½ teaspoon baking soda

3 tablespoons unsweetened cocoa powder

½ cup granulated sugar

3 tablespoons sunflower oil

1 teaspoon instant coffee, dissolved in 2 teaspoons boiling water

1½ teaspoons distilled white vinegar

to decorate

2 tablespoons sunflower oil

1½ tablespoons unsweetened cocoa powder

1 teaspoon instant coffee, dissolved in 2 tablespoons boiling water

1 cup confectioners' sugar, sifted

a 12-cup cupcake pan, lined with paper liners

makes 12

Preheat the oven to 350°F.

Combine the flour, baking soda, cocoa powder, and sugar and sift together into a bowl. Make a well in the center. Pour in ½ cup water, the oil, coffee, and vinegar and stir together.

Spoon the mixture into the paper liners and bake in the preheated oven for about 15 minutes until risen and firm and a skewer inserted in the center comes out clean. Transfer to a wire rack to cool.

To decorate, put the oil, cocoa powder, and coffee in a heatproof bowl set over a pan of gently simmering water and stir. Do not let the bowl touch the water. Gradually pour in the sugar and stir for about 2 minutes until thick and glossy. Add about ½ teaspoon more water to thin slightly and stir for another minute, then spoon the frosting over the cupcakes.

Warm, nutty, and fragrant with orange peel, these light, fluffy, gluten- and dairy-free cupcakes are plain and simple without being in the least bit dull. They melt in the mouth and are perfect served warm from the oven. For those who can't do without a little indulgence, serve them with a dollop of crème fraîche or cream on top.

ORANGE AND ALMOND CUPCAKES

2 eggs

7 tablespoons granulated sugar

grated peel of 1 unwaxed orange

¾ cup ground almonds

3 tablespoons potato flour

about ⅓ cup slivered almonds

confectioners' sugar, for dusting

a 12-cup cupcake pan, lined with paper liners

makes 12

Preheat the oven to 325°F.

Put the eggs and sugar in a bowl and beat for 5–10 minutes until thick and pale. Add the orange peel, then sift the ground almonds and potato flour into the mixture and fold in.

Spoon the mixture into the paper liners and sprinkle the slivered almonds over the top. Bake in the preheated oven for about 22 minutes until risen and golden and a skewer inserted in the center comes out clean. Transfer to a wire rack and let cool slightly before dusting with confectioners' sugar and serving.

These soft, chewy, egg-free cupcakes topped with a sweet and zesty cream cheese frosting are based on a classic muffin mixture and best eaten on the day you make them. Kids love them, so they're a great choice if you know a child with an egg allergy. Just remember to check they're not allergic to nuts.

BANANA, HONEY, AND PECAN CUPCAKES

1¼ cups self-rising flour

½ teaspoon baking powder

generous ⅓ cup shelled pecans, chopped

2 ripe bananas

3 tablespoons sunflower oil

4 tablespoons honey

¼ cup milk

to decorate

5 oz. cream cheese

⅓ cup confectioners' sugar, sifted

1 teaspoon freshly squeezed lime juice

slivered pecans, to decorate

a 12-cup cupcake pan, lined with paper liners

makes 12

Preheat the oven to 350°C.

Combine the flour and baking powder and sift into a bowl. Add the pecans and stir together. Make a well in the center.

In a separate bowl, mash the bananas with a fork. Add the oil, honey, and milk and stir together. Tip the mixture into the dry ingredients and stir together until just combined. (Don't overmix.)

Spoon the mixture into the paper liners and bake in the preheated oven for 20 minutes until risen and golden and skewer inserted in the center comes out clean. Transfer to a wire rack to cool.

To decorate, beat together the cream cheese, sugar, and lime juice until smooth and creamy, then swirl on top of the cupcakes. Decorate with slivered pecans.

With half the fat of a classic cupcake, these tempting little devils offer you a cupcake treat but with half the guilt attached. The prune and Armagnac purée stirred into the cupcakes gives them a distinctive flavor and moist texture. They're ideal for those with a sweet tooth who also like a little alcoholic kick in their desserts.

PRUNE AND ARMAGNAC CUPCAKES

2 oz. pitted prunes (dried plums)

3 tablespoons boiling water

1 tablespoon Armagnac or brandy

4 tablespoons unsalted butter, at room temperature

generous ¼ cup packed brown sugar

1 egg, beaten

1 cup self-rising flour

½ teaspoon baking powder

to decorate

1⅔ cups confectioners' sugar, sifted

2 tablespoons freshly squeezed lemon juice

12 pitted prunes (dried plums)

a 12-cup cupcake pan, lined with paper liners

makes 12

Preheat the oven to 350°C.

Put the prunes and boiling water in a blender and blend to make a purée. (Don't worry if it's not entirely smooth.) Set aside to cool, then stir in the Armagnac.

Beat together the butter and sugar, then stir in the prune purée. Beat in the egg, a little at a time, then sift the flour and baking powder into the mixture and fold in.

Spoon the mixture into the paper liners and bake in the preheated oven for about 18 minutes until golden and a skewer inserted in the center comes out clean. Transfer to a wire rack to cool.

To decorate, stir together the sugar and lemon juice until smooth, then spoon on top of the cupcakes. Top each one with a prune.

Not so much cupcakes as cup-meringues, these pretty little confections are nut- and gluten-free as well as being very low in fat. And the bittersweet chocolate drizzled on top is suitable for people on a dairy-free diet too. So whether you're dieting or suffering from food allergies, these are cupcakes that everyone can enjoy.

MERINGUE SPRINKLE CUPCAKES

2 egg whites

½ cup superfine sugar

to decorate

1 oz. bittersweet chocolate, chopped

sprinkles

a 12-cup cupcake pan, lined with paper liners

makes 12

Preheat the oven to 300°F.

Put the egg whites in a spotlessly clean bowl and beat until they stand in peaks. Sprinkle over a tablespoonful of sugar and beat in. Continue beating in the sugar a tablespoonful at a time until the egg whites are thick and glossy.

Using two tablespoons, shape the meringue into balls and drop into the paper lines. Bake in the preheated oven for 10 minutes, then reduce the temperature to 275°F and bake for a further 40 minutes. Turn off the oven but leave the meringues in the oven to cool.

To decorate, put the chocolate in a heatproof bowl set over a pan of gently simmering water. Do not let the bowl touch the water. Leave until melted, then drizzle over the meringues and scatter over some sprinkles.

These little cupcakes are considerably lower in fat than a classic coffee and walnut cake and yet they taste just as delicious. They are made with a light, butter-free cake batter and the ricotta frosting contains about one-eighth of the fat of a classic buttercream. Super easy to throw together, they are the perfect choice for afternoon tea.

COFFEE AND WALNUT CUPCAKES

2 eggs

¼ cup granulated sugar

1 teaspoon instant coffee, dissolved in 1 teaspoon boiling water

generous ½ cup all-purpose flour

to decorate

3 oz. ricotta

¼ cup confectioners' sugar, sifted

½ teaspoon instant coffee, dissolved in ½ teaspoon boiling water

12 walnut halves

a 12-cup cupcake pan, lined with paper liners

makes 12

Preheat the oven to 350°C.

Put the eggs and sugar in a bowl and beat for about 10 minutes until pale and thick. Drizzle the coffee into the mixture and fold in using a large metal spoon. Sift the flour into a separate bowl, then sift into the mixture and fold in.

Spoon the mixture into the paper liners and bake in the preheated oven for 12 minutes until risen and golden and a skewer inserted in the center comes out clean. Transfer to a wire rack to cool.

To decorate, beat together the ricotta, sugar, and coffee until smooth and creamy, then spoon on top of the cupcakes and top each one with a walnut half.

KIDS' CUPCAKES

You can't get much cuter than a plateful of these pink piggies sitting on the tea table. Except perhaps a gang of mini-farmers in checked shirts and matching overalls! So why not go with the animal theme and throw a farmyard tea party? Decorating these cupcakes is a little fiddly, but the final result is well worth the effort!

PINK PIGGY CUPCAKES

1 stick unsalted butter, at room temperature

½ cup granulated sugar

2 eggs

1 cup self-rising flour

1 teaspoon pure vanilla extract

2 tablespoons milk

to decorate

red food coloring

13 oz. ready-to-roll fondant icing

2 tablespoons raspberry jelly, sieved

dark purple or black food paste coloring

a 12-cup cupcake pan, lined with paper liners

three cookie cutters, one about the same size as your cupcake liners, one slightly smaller, and one very small

makes 12

Preheat the oven to 350°F.

Beat the butter and sugar together until pale and fluffy, then beat in the eggs, one at a time. Sift the flour into the mixture and fold in, then stir in the vanilla extract and milk.

Spoon the mixture into the paper liners and bake in the preheated oven for about 17 minutes until risen and golden and a skewer inserted into the center comes out clean. Transfer to a wire rack to cool.

To decorate, add a couple of drops of red food coloring to the fondant icing and knead until well blended to make a pale pink icing. Roll out the icing between two sheets of waxed paper or plastic wrap to about ¼ inch thick. Stamp out 12 rounds using the largest cookie cutter. Using a pastry brush, brush the tops of the cupcakes with jelly and gently press the pink rounds on top.

Using the scraps, roll out 12 rounds with the medium-sized cookie cutter, brush one side with water, and stick onto the cupcakes. Then with the smallest cutter, stamp out 12 rounds of icing and brush one side with water. Place in the center of each cupcake to make a nose and press gently in place. Using a round skewer, make two round holes next to each other for nostrils.

Using the remaining scraps of icing, cut out 24 small oval shapes for ears then brush the back of each lightly with water and fix two in place on top of each piggy's head, turning the tips of the ears up slightly. Roll a little icing into corkscrew tails and stick on.

Dip the flat end of a wooden skewer in the purple or black paste coloring. Dab two eyes above the nose, then draw a little mouth under the nose. Voilà!

Children will love learning to count with these fun number cupcakes with a sweet fruity crumb. You need to make the number decorations the day before to give them time to harden, so allow plenty of time to prepare ahead. This recipe suggests using three colors for the icing and numbers but you can use as many as you like.

NUMBER CUPCAKES

1 stick unsalted butter, at room temperature

½ cup granulated sugar

2 eggs

1 cup self-rising flour

4 oz. dried fruit

to decorate

1¾ oz. ready-to-roll fondant icing

yellow food coloring

green food coloring

⅔ cup mascarpone

½ cup confectioners' sugar, sifted

1 teaspoon freshly squeezed lemon juice

blue food coloring

a 12-cup cupcake pan, lined with paper liners

mini-number cookie cutters

makes 12

First make the number decorations. Divide the fondant icing into two pieces. Add a couple of drops of yellow food coloring to one piece and green to the other and knead until the colors are well blended. Roll out each piece between two sheets of waxed paper or plastic wrap to about ¼ inch thick. Stamp out as many numbers as you like using the cookie cutters. Let dry overnight until hard.

Preheat the oven to 350°F.

Beat the butter and sugar together until pale and fluffy, then beat in the eggs, one at a time. Sift the flour into the mixture and fold in, then stir in the dried fruit.

Spoon the mixture into the paper liners and bake in the preheated oven for 17 minutes until risen and golden and a skewer inserted in the center comes out clean. Transfer to a wire rack to cool.

To decorate, put the mascarpone, sugar, and lemon juice in a bowl and beat together until smooth and creamy. Add a few drops of blue food coloring and stir in until evenly mixed. Spread the icing on top of the cupcakes and stick the numbers into the icing so they stand up slightly.

These pretty spotty cupcakes look incredibly professional but are so easy to make. You can use plain round cookie cutters, or crinkle-cut ones which will give a pretty flowery effect. And of course, it's up to you which colors you use—you can easily adapt the recipe to match a party theme or color scheme.

SPOTTY CUPCAKES

1 stick unsalted butter, at room temperature

½ cup granulated sugar

2 eggs

1 cup self-rising flour

1 teaspoon pure vanilla extract

2 tablespoons milk

to decorate

1 lb. ready-to-roll fondant icing

red food coloring

green food coloring

2 tablespoons apricot jelly, sieved

a 12-cup cupcake pan, lined with paper liners

a cookie cutter, 2½ inches in diameter

a cookie cutter, ¾ inch in diameter

makes 12

Preheat the oven to 350°F.

Beat the butter and sugar together in a bowl until pale and fluffy, then beat in the eggs, one at a time. Sift the flour into the mixture and fold in, then stir in the vanilla extract and milk.

Spoon the mixture into the paper liners and bake in the preheated oven for about 17 minutes until risen and golden and a skewer inserted in the center comes out clean. Transfer to a wire rack to cool.

To decorate, divide the fondant icing into two pieces. Add a couple of drops of red food coloring to one piece and green to the other and knead until the colors are well blended. Roll out each piece between two sheets of waxed paper or plastic wrap to about ¼ inch thick, and large enough so that you will be able to cut out six rounds from each piece using the larger cookie cutter.

Using the smaller cookie cutter, cut rounds from the two sheets of icing—spacing them about ½ inch apart—to create a spotty pattern. Very carefully, without tearing the icing, remove the pink rounds and swap them with the green rounds so you end up with two pink and green spotty sheets of icing. Gently go over the icing with the rolling pin until it's about ¼ inch thick.

Using the larger cookie cutter, stamp out six rounds from each sheet. Brush the top of each cupcake with apricot jelly, then gently lay a round on top and pat in place.

These cute cupcakes topped with a smooth, creamy, not-too-sweet mascarpone frosting look like little hedgehogs. Get the kids to help out decorating the cupcakes—they'll just love sticking the chocolate chips into the creamy frosting. They make a nice change from chocolate chip cookies as a little treat after school.

CHOCOLATE CHIP CUPCAKES

1 stick unsalted butter, at room temperature

½ cup granulated sugar

2 eggs

1 cup self-rising flour

1 teaspoon pure vanilla extract

½ cup bittersweet chocolate chips

to decorate

⅔ cup mascarpone

⅓ cup confectioners' sugar, sifted

¼ teaspoon pure vanilla extract

2 tablespoons bittersweet chocolate chips, chilled

a 12-cup cupcake pan, lined with paper liners

makes 12

Preheat the oven to 350°F.

Beat the butter and sugar together in a bowl until pale and fluffy, then beat in the eggs, one at a time. Sift the flour into the mixture and fold in, then stir in the vanilla extract. Sprinkle over the chocolate chips and fold in.

Spoon the mixture into the paper liners and bake in the preheated oven for about 17 minutes until risen and golden and a skewer inserted in the center comes out clean. Transfer to a wire rack to cool.

To decorate, put the mascarpone, sugar, and vanilla extract in a bowl and beat together until smooth and creamy. Spread the frosting on the cupcakes, then carefully press the chocolate chips on top of the cupcakes like little hedgehog spines. (Handle the chocolate chips as little as possible to avoid them melting.)

Just like a batch of sugary little treasure chests, these pretty bejeweled cupcakes will appeal to girly girls—but cheeky little pirates won't be able to keep their hands off them either! Make sure you break the hard candies into small enough pieces so that they aren't a choking hazard for small children.

HIDDEN TREASURE CUPCAKES

1 stick unsalted butter, at room temperature

½ cup granulated sugar

2 eggs

1 cup self-rising flour

grated peel of 1 unwaxed orange

3 tablespoons candied peel (optional)

to decorate

4½ oz. fruit-flavor hard candies in their wrappers

⅔ cup confectioners' sugar, sifted

1 tablespoon freshly squeezed lemon juice

orange food coloring

a 12-cup cupcake pan, lined with paper liners

makes 12

Preheat the oven to 350°F.

Beat the butter and sugar together in a bowl until pale and fluffy, then beat in the eggs, one at a time. Sift the flour into the mixture and fold in, then stir in the orange peel and candied peel, if using.

Spoon the mixture into the paper liners and bake in the preheated oven for 17 minutes until golden and a skewer inserted in the center comes out clean. Transfer to a wire rack to cool.

To decorate, leaving the candies in their wrappers, hit them with a rolling pin to break into large pieces. (Don't smash them into dust!) Tip the broken candies into a bowl and set aside.

Stir together the sugar and lemon juice and add a couple of drops of the food coloring to make an orange icing. Spoon the icing onto the cupcakes and pile the broken candy "jewels" on top.

These cupcakes are perfect for serving as dessert for a party—but they can be messy so be sure to have plenty of napkins at the ready for wiping up sticky fingers! I like vanilla ice cream with mine, but you can choose any flavor you like—chocolate, strawberry, and mint-choc-chip are always favorites.

ICE CREAM CUPCAKES

4 tablespoons unsalted butter, at room temperature

¼ cup granulated sugar

1 egg, beaten

generous ⅓ cup self-rising flour

to decorate

2 oz. bittersweet chocolate, chopped

2½ tablespoons heavy cream

1 tablespoon corn syrup

ice cream

a 12-cup cupcake pan, lined with paper liners

makes 12

Preheat the oven to 350°F.

Beat the butter and sugar in a bowl until pale and fluffy, then gradually beat in the egg. Sift the flour into the mixture and fold in.

Spoon the mixture into the paper liners and bake in the preheated oven for about 15 minutes until risen and golden and a skewer inserted in the center comes out clean. Transfer to a wire rack and let cool completely. When they've cooled, use a serrated knife to carefully cut a shallow hole out of the center of the cupcakes. Keep what you've cut out for lids.

To decorate, put the chocolate, cream, and syrup in a small saucepan and warm gently, stirring, until the chocolate starts to melt. Remove the pan from the heat and continue stirring until smooth and creamy and the chocolate has completely melted.

Using a melon baller, make small scoops of ice cream and place on top of the cupcakes. Replace the lids of the cupcakes, then spoon over the chocolate sauce and serve immediately.

These pretty pink cupcakes with a jelly-rippled crumb are always a hit with kids. If your kids want to decorate the cupcakes themselves, you might want to leave off the piped spirals—but they'll look just as lovely simply topped with raspberries. They're also gorgeous for adults to give to a loved one as a token of their affection.

RASPBERRY RIPPLE CUPCAKES

1 stick unsalted butter, at room temperature

½ cup granulated sugar

2 eggs

1 cup self-rising flour

2 tablespoons raspberry jelly

to decorate

1 cup confectioners' sugar, sifted

1–1½ tablespoons freshly squeezed lemon juice

red food coloring

12 raspberries

a 12-cup cupcake pan, line with paper liners

a piping bag, fitted with a narrow tip

makes 12

Preheat the oven to 350°F.

Beat the butter and sugar together in a bowl until pale and fluffy, then beat in the eggs, one at a time. Sift the flour into the mixture and fold in.

Put the jelly in a small bowl and stir well until runny. Spoon dollops of the cake mixture into the paper liners and flatten slightly with the back of a teaspoon, making a slight indent in the center. Drop about ¼ teaspoon jelly in the center of each indent. Top with the remaining cake mixture and drizzle about ¼ teaspoon more jelly on top of each one. Draw a skewer through each cupcake about three times to ripple the mixture. Bake in the preheated oven for about 18 minutes until risen and golden. Transfer to a wire rack to cool.

To decorate, put the sugar in a bowl and gradually stir in the lemon juice until you have a thick, spooning consistency. Reserve a couple of tablespoonfuls of the icing, then add one or two drops of red food coloring to the remaining icing. Stir well until you have your desired color.

Spoon the icing onto the cupcakes. Spoon the reserved white icing into the piping bag fitted with a narrow tip. Pipe a white spiral onto each cupcake, then put a raspberry in the center of each one.

suppliers and stockists

Beaucoup Wedding Favors
www.beau-coup.com
Tel: 877-988-2328
Carries the hard-to-find Italian silver "amorini" chocolate hearts or mini pastel hearts, which are perfect for decorating Valentine cupcakes.

Confectionery House
www.confectioneryhouse.com
Tel: 518-279-4250
Paper liners in every color for every occasion as well as sprinkles and other edible decorations.

www.coolcupcakes.com
Tel: 1-800-797-2887
Perfect stop for baking enthusiasts and the cupcake-obsessed looking for sanding sugar, edible glitter, and sprinkles in a rainbow of colors, plus great paper liners and three-, four-, five- and six-tier cupcake stands.

Crate & Barrel
www.crateandbarrel.com
Tel: 800-967-6696
Cupcake pans, cute cupcake baking gift set, and holiday cupcake stencils for the true cupcake fanatic!

Into the Oven
www.intotheoven.com
For rolled fondant icing, dragées, edible glitter dust, and other baking supplies from around the world.

King Arthur Flour
www.kingarthurflour.com
Tel: 800-827-6836
Anyone hoping to transport cupcakes needs a sturdy plastic carrier from The Bakers Catalogue to keep their cakes safe from the rough and tumble of any trip—to the potluck, the school party, or a picnic. The site is an excellent resource all baking supplies.

Kitchen Krafts
www.kitchenkrafts.com
Tel: 800-298-5389
The Foodcrafters Supply Catalog carries hard-to-find edible gold dragées, cupcake stands, fun seasonal paper liners, food coloring etc.

Nordic Ware
www.nordicware.com
Tel: 1-877-466-7342
Family-owned, American bakeware manufacturer offers the Heartlette Dessert Pan for baking heart-shape cupcakes.

Williams-Sonoma
www.williams-sonoma.com
Tel: 877-812-6235
Beautiful selection of cupcake-related items, including monogrammed cupcake gift boxes, holiday silicone cupcake molds, and nonstick pans.

Wilton
www.wilton.com
Professional cake decorators know Wilton, and baking enthusiasts at every level will enjoy browsing their online store.

index

conversion chart

Weights and measures have been rounded up
or down slightly to make measuring easier.

Measuring butter:
A US stick of butter weighs 4 oz. which is
approximately 115 g or 8 tablespoons.

The recipes in this book require the
following conversions:

American	Metric	Imperial
6 tbsp	85 g	3 oz.
7 tbsp	100 g	3½ oz.
1 stick	115 g	4 oz.

Volume equivalents:

American	Metric	Imperial
1 teaspoon	5 ml	
1 tablespoon	15 ml	
¼ cup	60 ml	2 fl. oz.
⅓ cup	75 ml	2½ fl. oz.
½ cup	125 ml	4 fl. oz.
⅔ cup	150 ml	5 fl. oz. (¼ pint)
¾ cup	175 ml	6 fl. oz.
1 cup	250 ml	8 fl. oz.

Weight equivalents:		Measurements:	
Imperial	Metric	Inches	cm
1 oz.	30 g	¼ inch	5 mm
2 oz.	55 g	½ inch	1 cm
3 oz.	85 g	1 inch	2.5 cm
3½ oz.	100 g	2 inches	5 cm
4 oz.	115 g	3 inches	7 cm
6 oz.	175 g	4 inches	10 cm
8 oz. (½ lb.)	225 g	5 inches	12 cm
9 oz.	250 g	6 inches	15 cm
10 oz.	280 g	7 inches	18 cm
12 oz.	350 g	8 inches	20 cm
13 oz.	375 g	9 inches	23 cm
14 oz.	400 g	10 inches	25 cm
15 oz.	425 g	11 inches	28 cm
16 oz. (1 lb.)	450 g	12 inches	30 cm

Oven temperatures:

120°C	(250°F)	Gas ½
140°C	(275°F)	Gas 1
150°C	(300°F)	Gas 2
170°C	(325°F)	Gas 3
180°C	(350°F)	Gas 4
190°C	(375°F)	Gas 5
200°C	(400°F)	Gas 6
220°C	(425°F)	Gas 7